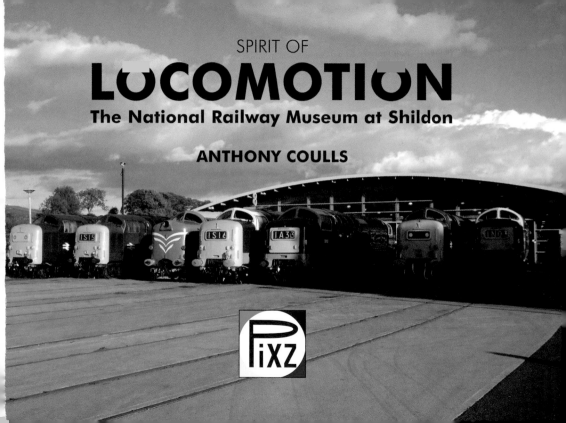

SPIRIT OF
LOCOMOTION
The National Railway Museum at Shildon

ANTHONY COULLS

First published in Great Britain in 2012
Copyright text and photographs © 2012 Anthony
Coulls.

*Title page: 50 years of Deltic locomotives was
celebrated on 7-8 October 2011 with a gathering
of all 7 surviving locomotives including the Prototype
Deltic from 1955.*

*Below: 1247, the first locomotive to be preserved by
a private individual, Capt. Bill Smith, had a repaint into
original colours in 2008 and is seen in May that year
fresh out of the workshop.*

British Library Cataloguing-in-Publication Data
A CIP record for this title is available from the
British Library

ISBN 978 0 85710 064 1

PiXZ Books
Halsgrove House, Ryelands Business Park,
Bagley Road, Wellington, Somerset TA21 9PZ
Tel: 01823 653777, Fax: 01823 216796
email: sales@halsgrove.com

An imprint of Halstar Ltd, part of the
Halsgrove group of companies
Information on all Halsgrove titles is available
at: www.halsgrove.com

Printed and bound in China by
Toppan Leefung Printing Ltd

Introduction

Entering Shildon by road, the town name signs say "Cradle of the Railways". Until 2004, any visitor to the town would have been forgiven for wondering what that meant. Since that year, the reason has been made explicit with the creation of Locomotion – The National Railway Museum at Shildon.

The town's long association with railways began in the 1820s, when the new Stockton & Darlington Railway chose the town for its engineering headquarters, and on 27 September 1825, George Stephenson's "Locomotion" set off from outside the Mason's Arms public house hauling the first train from Stockton and imprinting the location in railway history. In 1827, an engineer named Timothy Hackworth was appointed to look after the company's locomotives and made his home in the town. As time progressed, he established his own locomotive works as well as the Stockton & Darlington one, and after his death in 1851, Shildon began to carve a niche as the major wagon works for the S&DR, then later the North Eastern Railway, London &

North Eastern Railway and finally British Railways. With industrial growth and prosperity from local coal mines contributing to the town, a network of railway lines criss crossed the settlement, but it was those links with earliest times that remained in the local psyche and being the reason by which the town became best known.

Over the years, Shildon's railway heritage was recognised by being the location where 150 years of the Stockton & Darlington Railway were celebrated in 1975 with an exhibition of rolling stock and a cavalcade of locomotives along the line to Heighington. A small museum was set up and opened by the Queen Mother, and there matters rested until 1983 when the wagon works were threatened with closure. The whole raison d'etre for the town was under threat, but a combination of political pressure and lack of orders resulted in its eventual closure after a long fight in 1984 with the loss of some 2,900 jobs. An amount of re-investment saw some new opportunities

created, but for nearly 20 years, Shildon became somewhere that very few had heard of and even fewer visited.

Enter the National Railway Museum. In the late 1990s, the National Railway Museum decided to get to grips with its vast collection and make it more accessible if at all possible. At the main museum site in York, the small objects were placed in open store in what is known as The Warehouse. Museum managers sought to do the same with the rolling stock, some 70 items of which were in inadequate store either at York or elsewhere across the country. The NRM's head, Andrew Scott, went out to the public and private sector, looking for partnerships to develop what was initially conceived as a major storage facility for the rolling stock collection, with occasional public access days. Many locations were examined, but at Shildon in County Durham, Sedgefield Borough Council offered a brown field site, with a long rail history and connected to the national rail network in a

2006 marked the 40th anniversary of the end of the Tyne Dock-Consett iron ore trains. For the occasion, "Black Prince" carried the identity of its long gone classmates at the Annual Steam Gala.

partnership that offered the most potential for both parties.

Thus it was that "Shildon Railway Village" came into planning. Envisaged as an accessible store shed, it quickly morphed into a full tourist attraction of a museum, encompassing the old Timothy Hackworth Museum and historic buildings surrounding it, but including a new Collections Facility linked by ⅔ mile of railway line upon which steam rides could be given and visitors reach both ends of the site. Daily opening became an option and visitor facilities were included. As planning moved to groundwork and construction began, the name was changed to "Locomotion – the National Railway Museum at Shildon" giving the new museum a much higher profile brand and location.

At the historic end of the site, a core cluster of buildings was refurbished – including Soho House, Hackworth's own home. A former Sunday School building was renovated to become the Welcome Centre for the new museum, and Hackworth's original "Sans Pareil" locomotive installed as a centrepiece – a task which entailed partial removal of a wall to get the locomotive inside. Railway works cottages became museum offices, and the oldest industrial building in Shildon, the Soho shed, was renovated to house the National Railway Museum's collection of early coal-carrying chaldron wagons and other related relics in a suitable setting. General site clearance enhanced the appearance of the imposing coal drops, last used for coaling locomotives in 1935, and the Black Boy railway horse stables were protected and consolidated, pending a full restoration in the fullness of time. The old goods shed was cleaned, repainted and the interior whitewashed in readiness for its new role as starting point for the railway steam rides along the site's running line to the new building housing the rail vehicle collection. As one continues down the site, the line follows the course of the original Stockton and Darlington route and passes the current Shildon station, which retains a few original buildings and the mechanical signal box – one of the last remaining ones in the North East still in its original location and in use. At one point, there are four historic rail routes within yards of each other, giving an impression of the importance of the railways to the area.

The site of the Collections building itself was, in the pre-1914 period, claimed to be the "largest railway sidings in the world" and postcards to this effect were sold! There were 27 sidings, stretching for nearly a mile in the Newton Aycliffe direction. From 1915 to 1935, the line was electrified – one of the North Eastern Railway's innovations. As coal traffic lessened, steam power returned and the sidings contracted, but were still in place right to the end of the wagon works. In 1975, part of the sidings site was the location for the grandstands for the cavalcade visitors — and now on the spot stands a modern purpose-built steel-framed display hall, spanning seven tracks.

During the spring of 2004, track began to be laid and in June 2004, the first locomotives arrived on the museum site — a humble class 03 diesel shunter and an LNER Q7 goods engine. A gathering of sponsors, partners and local dignitaries watched the latter being installed into the new Collections building and then the hard work began — with the new museum due to open on 25 September (as close to the Stockton & Darlington anniversary as possible), nearly 70 locomotives, carriages and wagons to install, plus museum displays to fit out and offices, shop and café to equip, the race against time was on!

Suffice it to say, the deadline was met, and on the first open weekend, thousands came to see what it was all about, far exceeding the numbers expected. This was a soft opening however, and the official opening happened a month later on 22 October, when a special train worked up from York hauled by the steam loco "Duchess of Sutherland". In front of VIPs, local dignitaries, funders, staff and volunteers and in the company of NRM flagships "Flying Scotsman" and "City of Truro", the then Prime Minister and MP for Sedgefield, Tony Blair declared the museum open before taking part in a tour of the new museum and placing it firmly on the map.

In the first 12 months of opening, 210,000 visitors took advantage of the chance to visit, whereas it had been anticipated that 60,000 would come. From an early date, the museum began to establish a programme of innovative and exciting events, tying in the unique heritage of the region with the appeal of the North East's first National Museum. Thus it is that model railway shows sit alongside classic car displays and the annual Steam Gala now attracts regular attendance of over 10,000 visitors. At least 70,000 visitors per year now come for these events alone according to surveys. A number of events have become fixtures and are eagerly anticipated, whilst others have come and gone — always keeping the offer fresh and giving a varied experience through the year. In 2010, the museum played host to the new-build express steam locomotive "Tornado" and in 2011 held a one-off event to celebrate the 50th anniversary of

2011's visiting locomotive for the season was Manning Wardle "Sir Berkeley" from the Vintage Carriages Trust and the Middleton Railway. Here raising steam in September that year.

the Deltic diesel locomotive, where all six surviving production Deltics were lined up alongside the prototype locomotive, a long-term resident of the Shildon museum. Every two years, the museum is host to the Guild of Railway Artists' "Railart", a prestigious event looked forward to by many.

The events support a selection of now over 70 vehicles from the National Collection. It has become the policy for the display to be a dynamic one, for Locomotion is a working museum. Some vehicles have been on site for nearly 8 years since the opening, others come for a matter of days and, in between, the museum team have tried to ensure that many of the stars of the National Collection have been or are on display at Shildon. Since opening, the museum has played host to "Evening Star", "Green Arrow", the working replica of "Rocket", "City of Truro", "Flying Scotsman" and most recently "Mallard" paid a visit for 12 months. Many other locomotives, carriages and wagons have been exchanged between Shildon, York and other heritage railways and museums, ensuring that a return visit to Locomotion is never the same. Privately-owned or heritage-railway-owned locomotives have also been hired in over the years to work the site's passenger steam shuttle service, though as time has passed, some folk are now keen to have diesel hauled trains by the resident shunting locomotives which are fitted with brakes to allow

A local London & North Eastern Railway theme in April 2010 with "Green Arrow" and new-build class A1 "Tornado" parked on the sidings during a Giants of Steam event.

them to work passenger trips. A dedicated team of volunteers supports the staff in running the railway, whilst others give up their spare time to clean exhibits, raise funds or publicise the museum at external events.

In 2011, a new venture was the running of special trains between the National Railway Museum's main site at York and Shildon on two consecutive weekends – the second of which included steam galas at both sites. With the trains headed by historic steam and diesel locomotives, the operations cemented the link between the two NRM sites in a physical way that had not been tapped into beforehand, and paved the way for future services of this type.

The museum's main Collections building has a two track conservation workshop built in to the fabric, and this is fully viewable from the main exhibition area. Since 2006, there have been trainees working under a manager in the workshop, repairing and restoring historic railway vehicles. The first to be restored was a small locomotive called "Woolmer", which arrived in pieces, and after careful reassembly and repair is now on display at the Milestones Museum in Basingstoke, Hampshire.

The trainees have been able to learn new skills from fabrication, turning, welding and riveting to coachpainting and signwriting – all very valuable indeed in the growing heritage sector. There is a ready market for trained people from the younger generation, and the National Railway Museum is committed to furthering the sustainability of the collection by ensuring its competent care.

Since its opening, Locomotion has established itself as one of the biggest tourist attractions in the North East. It has re-established Shildon as a venue to be visited, and plays a key part in the local economy. Many of the staff come from Shildon or close by and are from families with a background in the railway industry. A key policy has always been to use local suppliers and support business wherever possible – and many townsfolk are regular visitors, coming to see what's new. As the museum moves towards having been open ten years, the team look towards new challenges and opportunities to refresh the attraction and build on the successes of recent years – and it is our hope that you will enjoy this illustrated celebration of those years and share the enjoyment that has gone into the museum so far.

A preservation pioneer was Great Northern J52 loco 68846, since repainted at Shildon in GNR livery and returned to York for display, seen here in 2004 not long after the museum opened to the public.

Opposite: A rare outing into the November sun in 2005 for the sole surviving North Staffordshire Railway steam loco, 0-6-2 tank No. 2 and the first time it had been out of the County of Staffordshire during its preservation life.

A major project is to reunite Stirling Single No.1 with the correct tender which it has been without for over 100 years. This photo was taken with the new tender to publicise the project in January 2011.

A stalwart of the shunting yards at Shildon were the J72 class locomotives. Number 69023 of the type visited in 2010 and brought back memories of sister engines moving trucks around until the 1960s.

Opposite: A regular feature of July each year is the Shildon Classic Car show – and it grows every time, filling the site.

A relic from the earlier days of steam railways was Hetton Lyon, dating from 1851. Always based in the North East, it is now on loan to Beamish as part of their waggonway display.

A visitor in 2011 was this privately owned 8F class locomotive
which had just been repatriated from Turkey. Its work-worn condition compared
to the pristine other exhibits has proved a major talking point.

Opposite: A working replica of Stephenson's "Planet" loco came to the 2009 Steam Gala
from the Science Museum at Manchester and gave rides in its appropriate coaches.

After 8 years of grafting reliably, the workshop team gave the 03 shunter a facelift in summer 2011 and turned it out in original British Railways green as D2090 as it was when new.

Opposite: Early events at the museum were goods train weekends; visiting P3 class No. 2392 does the honours on a set of wagons in June 2005.

After dark, the site takes on a different atmosphere and photo opportunities change. A National Carriers Scammell Townsman lines up alongside the NRM's Western diesel hydraulic locomotive for a photo evening.

Arguably the most famous of them all – A4 class "Mallard" spent a year at Shildon from June 2010, arriving hauled by "Tornado" and here about to be put on display after cleaning.

Above left: Apprentice Johnny Molloy works on fitting the jib to a Smith, Rodley steam crane under renovation in the Shildon conservation workshops.

Above right: At goods train weekends, a shunting engine puts together a bigger train for a large locomotive to take away. The P3 is seen from the cab of the shunting loco, "Matthew Murray".

As part of a Chinese Festival in 2008, a narrow gauge locomotive from China was displayed alongside a dragon. At that time, the locomotive was less than 20 years old!

Opposite: Diesel locomotives are now historic in their own right and find a place in the National Collection. This 1959 Sentinel worked for 50 years before joining the NRM.

Barclay Fireless Loco Imperial No.1 moved up from York in October 2005; it worked at a paper mill where fires and flames would have been dangerous so was charged up with steam from a stationary boiler.

"Eustace Forth", a Newcastle-built tank engine arrived from York in May 2006 and was promptly steam tested for crew training. Here it is in the yard along with P3 No. 2392

Opposite: February frost highlights the massive bulk of the coal drops – the most imposing feature on the site, used until 1935 to coal locomotives shedded at Shildon.

Engines come and go – for three years from February 2007, this little London & North Western Railway tank locomotive was resident before moving to Preston.

The very first Anniversary Steam Gala line up in September 2005.

Great Western Railway 813 leaves Collection at the 2007 Steam Gala. Forty years earlier, it worked in the North East for the National Coal Board.

Like a scene from the 1970s or early 1980s, two blue diesels share solace in the snow of January 2008. 03 090 and 37 003 freeze it out!

In June 2008, Locomotion played host to the last steam locomotive built for British Railways, Class 9F "Evening Star", on its way to the STEAM museum at Swindon.

In September 2009, the Transport Trust recognised the legacy of Timothy Hackworth to Shildon, and presented a Red Wheel plaque to be fixed to Hackworth's old house. His great great granddaughter Jane Hackworth-Young receives the plaque from the Trust's Clive Morris.

In the cold February of 2008, the Beyer Peacock tank loco approaches the Goods Shed with a lightly loaded passenger shuttle.

Opposite: In September 2011, steam shuttles were run between York and Shildon. On 18 September, 6201 "Princess Elizabeth" waits to leave Shildon with a southbound train.

In the Soho shed on site at Shildon is a small collection of early railway rolling stock, headed here by a chaldron waggon from Cramlington Colliery dating from 1826.

Opposite: Just as locos arrive by main line, so they depart main line. 55 022 "Kings Own Yorkshire Light Infantry" takes the NRM's Western and 37 locos back to York early on an April morning after a successful Diesel Gala.

It is good to display vehicles doing the job they were built for – here a GWR motor car van displays preservation pioneer Tom Rolt's Alvis of 1927. Tom Rolt was involved in the first preserved railway in the world, the Talyllyn line in Mid Wales.

Let us not forget that thousands of industrial engines worked across the UK in mines, quarries and steelworks amongst other places. At Shildon, "Juno", a Hunslet of 1958 represents the thousands of these machines for the nation.

"Locomotion" at Locomotion – the 1975 replica from Beamish Museum made an appearance in May 2011 for the Early Days of Steam Gala.

Locomotion has attracted many interesting visiting locomotives – this is Manning Wardle tank engine "Matthew Murray" from the Middleton Railway in summer 2005.

Opposite: Low winter light in November 2005 catches 68846 and 563 during a "Cab It" event where visitors are able to visit the cabs of selected engines from the collection.

Locomotive namings are a pleasant diversion on occasions – in March 2009 this Freightliner class 66 freight loco was named "Stephenson Locomotive Society" for their centenary.

Making a rare appearance outside for a photographic session in November 2006 was "Cornwall" with its 8 foot diameter driving wheels. Originally built in 1848, it has had a long and chequered life.

Many locomotives have visited and run on the line at Shildon,
here Barclay 22 from Bowes Railway takes a turn on the
passenger service in the summer of 2006.

Of the many vehicles at Locomotion, perhaps this is the oddest! The 1947 Matisa track tamping machine gets a rare outing during a shunting operation in October 2009.

Opposite: The NRM's own Beattie well tank locomotive is seen about to leave the Goods Shed in August 2006 during a period of display and operation at Shildon.

A great number of volunteers work at Locomotion and here the APT-E support group work alongside museum engineering staff on stabilising the gas-turbine-powered tilting train that they care for.

On 2 November 2006, Robert Heath No. 6 from the Foxfield Railway was working a goods train for the benefit of a group of photographers.

One of the rarest engines in the Northern Hemisphere is this small Hunslet tank engine from the First World War, repatriated from Australia and making its UK debut appearance at Shildon in 2006. It has since moved on for restoration to working order.

One of the smaller guests at the 2005 Steam Gala was Sentinel "Anne" from the Embsay and Bolton Abbey Steam Railway.

Opposite: Principal guest at the first 2005 Steam Gala, Jubilee class "Leander", makes a demonstration run on the running line at Locomotion.

People often ask how things are moved around at Locomotion – here's the answer, the 03 diesel shunter is fitted with an exhaust cleaner, and is seen at work in October 2009.

RB004, a Leyland prototype railbus gets refuelled with diesel from a road tanker at the 2008 diesel gala. Its successors now work the main line railway past the site to Bishop Auckland.

Opposite: Unique Kitson-built "A No. 5" from North Tyneside Railway made a rare appearance away from home at the 2005 Steam Gala.

Shildon works built this working replica of "Sans Pareil" in 1979, and it starred in the 2005 Gala. Here it is raising steam alongside guest "A No. 5" from North Tyneside.

Shining in the September sun is "Mayflower", star guest at the 2007 Steam Gala and as clean as you can get a steam locomotive!

Above left: Steam in the snow is always a bit special and the replica of Hackworth's "Sans Pareil" provides a unique insight into the life of an 1820s' engine driver, with no cab for protection...

Above right: Synonymous with Shildon is the replica of Hackworth's "Sans Pareil", built in the town in 1979. It was given a cosmetic overhaul in authentic colours in the spring of 2009.

The 2011 Steam Gala had a Great Western Railway theme. Here tank engine 5643, heavy goods engine 2818 and "City of Truro" line up for the photographers.

Opposite: The Aveling & Porter traction engine type locomotive "Blue Circle" takes a slow trip past the coal drops on 18 March 2005.

The first Shildon restoration, "Woolmer" from the Longmoor Military Railway, was outshopped in November 2007, making a stark contrast with the unrestored Great Western Railway coach behind it.

The first visiting operating locomotive for 2004-2005 was "WST" from the Bowes Railway, here passing the coal drops. Driver Tony Newton has since emigrated to warmer climes in New Zealand!

Right: The hard frost of December 2009 brought out this amazing cobweb on the Great Northern tender for the Stirling Single loco from 1870.

The icon of the museum has been the prototype "Deltic" diesel electric from 1955, seen outside the museum when being measured to make a 00 gauge model.

Opposite: The North Eastern Locomotive Preservation Group has strong links with the museum, and their K1 class loco 62005 takes a run up the line in May 2010.

The museum works well with local partners, and in August 2008 began to run shuttle bus services with the Aycliffe & District Bus Preservation Society whose Bristol single decker is a TV star!

The North East has a long heritage of locomotive building, going back to 1805 and a Trevithick type loco. The bicentenary was celebrated in July 2005 in conjunction with the Tanfield Railway who sent their locomotive "No. 2" for display for the summer.

The North Eastern Railway was a pioneer of electric traction, electrifying the line at Shildon between 1915 and 1935. The heritage is reflected in the electric loco No.1 from 1904 which worked on the quayside at Newcastle.

The National Railway Museum has a twinning agreement with the NRM in Sierra Leone and for a time, a Sierra Leonean engine (now preserved in Wales) was on display at Shildon on a wagon suited to move it around site.

The NRM has good relationships with many heritage railways including the Severn Valley Railway, who lent Standard 4 Class No. 80079 for display in Spring 2005.

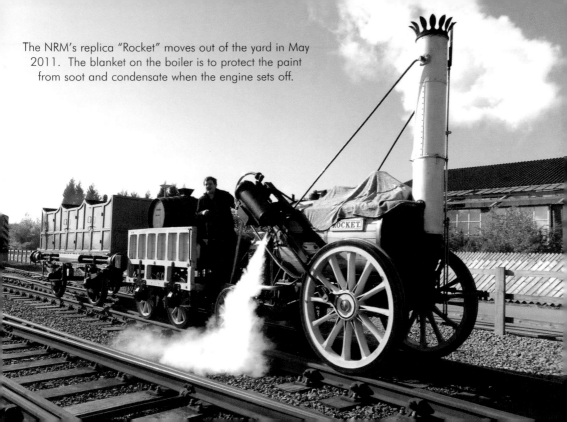

The NRM's replica "Rocket" moves out of the yard in May 2011. The blanket on the boiler is to protect the paint from soot and condensate when the engine sets off.

Above left: The October rally in 2005 was blessed with fine weather – just as well for this Wallis & Steevens traction engine has no roof!

Above right: The "Sans Pareil" replica lets off steam in October 2007 during a boiler test for the insurance company.

London Midland & Scottish Railway "Crab" in its new guise as 13000 was rolled out in December 2010 after a repaint and conservation and is good enough to use as a Christmas card!

Thousands came to the 2009 Steam Gala to see "Oliver Cromwell" which had arrived off the main line. The National Collection engine took part in a photo session at Locomotion on the Sunday morning as seen here.

Training in heritage skills has been a major factor in the museum since 2006.
Apprentice Johnny Molloy works on a steam crane not long
after starting work in September 2009.

Upon the end of its 10 year boiler ticket, LNER V2 "Green Arrow" moved from the North Yorkshire Moors Railway to Shildon for display. In 2010 it returned by rail to York.

Opposite: What it's all about! Sunshine and steam at the 2006 Steam Gala.

Wagons have a long connection with Shildon and in June 2006, 22 from Bowes takes the 300 ton boiler wagon set for a trip up the line on a goods train day.

Winter light at Shildon highlights Furness Railway No. 20 as it sets off to fetch the brake van for the Santa trains of December 2009.